COLOR TRACE LEARN

This book belongs to

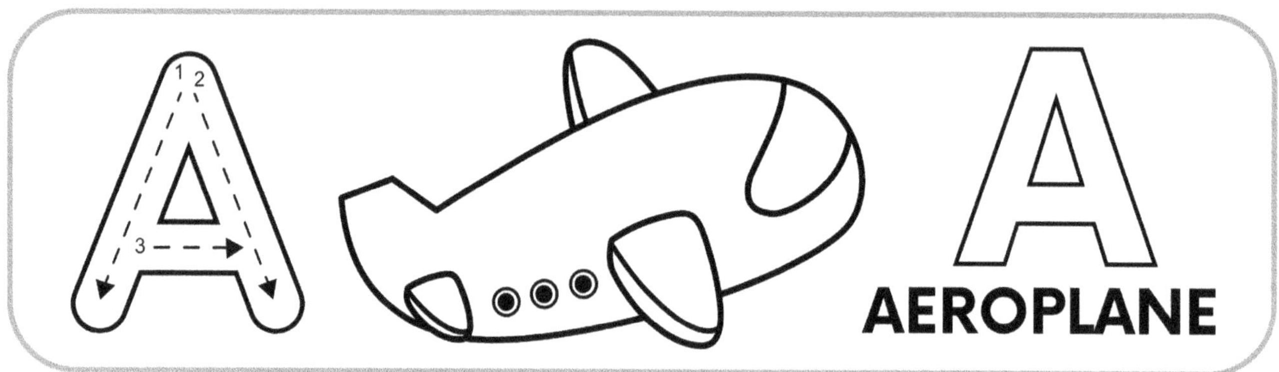

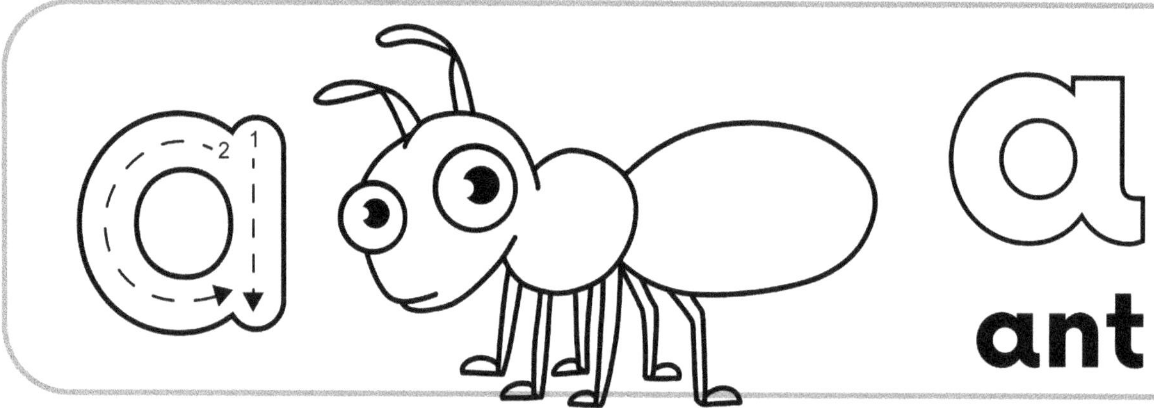

A A

AEROPLANE

a a

ant

Aa Aa Aa Aa Aa Aa Aa

Aa Aa Aa Aa Aa Aa Aa

Aa Aa Aa Aa Aa Aa Aa

Aa Aa Aa Aa Aa Aa Aa

Aa Aa Aa Aa Aa Aa Aa

Aa Aa Aa Aa Aa Aa Aa

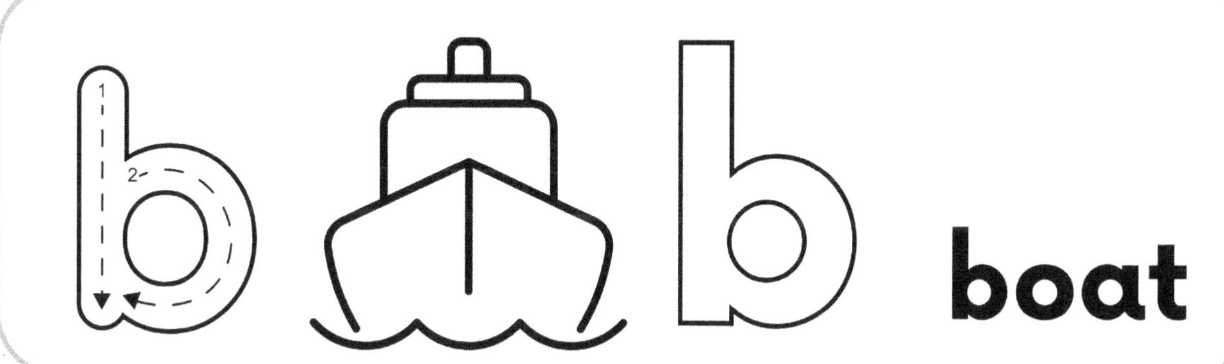

Bb Bb Bb Bb Bb Bb Bb

Bb Bb Bb Bb Bb Bb Bb

Bb Bb Bb Bb Bb Bb Bb

Bb Bb Bb Bb Bb Bb Bb

Bb Bb Bb Bb Bb Bb Bb

Bb Bb Bb Bb Bb Bb Bb

1
CAT
1
cake
Cc Cc Cc Cc Cc Cc Cc

D D **DOG**

d d **duck**

Dd dd Dd Dd Dd Dd Dd

Dd dd Dd Dd Dd Dd Dd

Dd dd Dd Dd Dd Dd Dd

Dd dd Dd Dd Dd Dd Dd

Dd dd Dd Dd Dd Dd Dd

Dd dd Dd Dd Dd Dd Dd

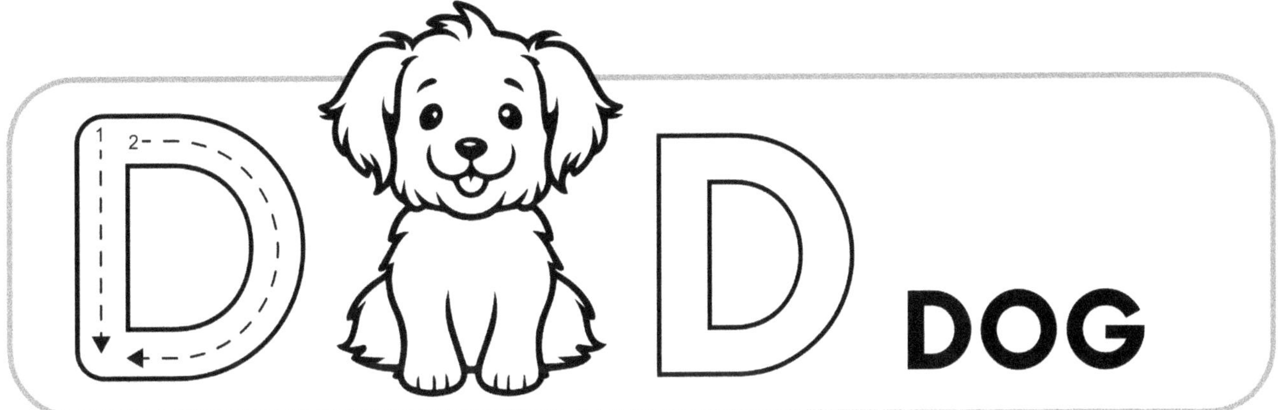

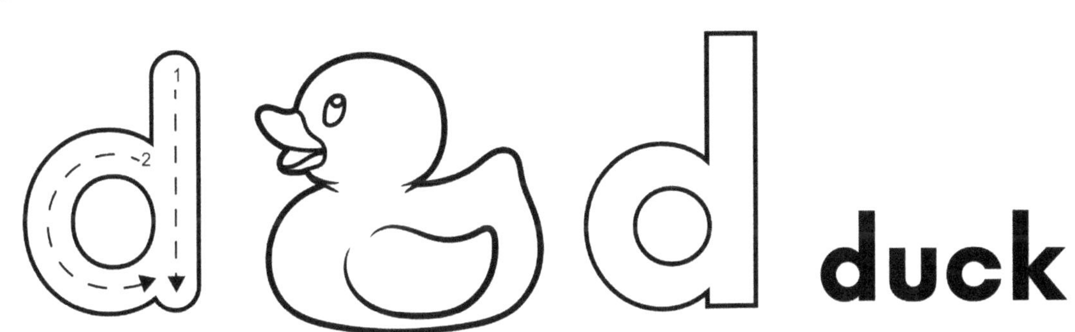

E
ELEPHANT
e
eagle

F
FLOWER

f
fish

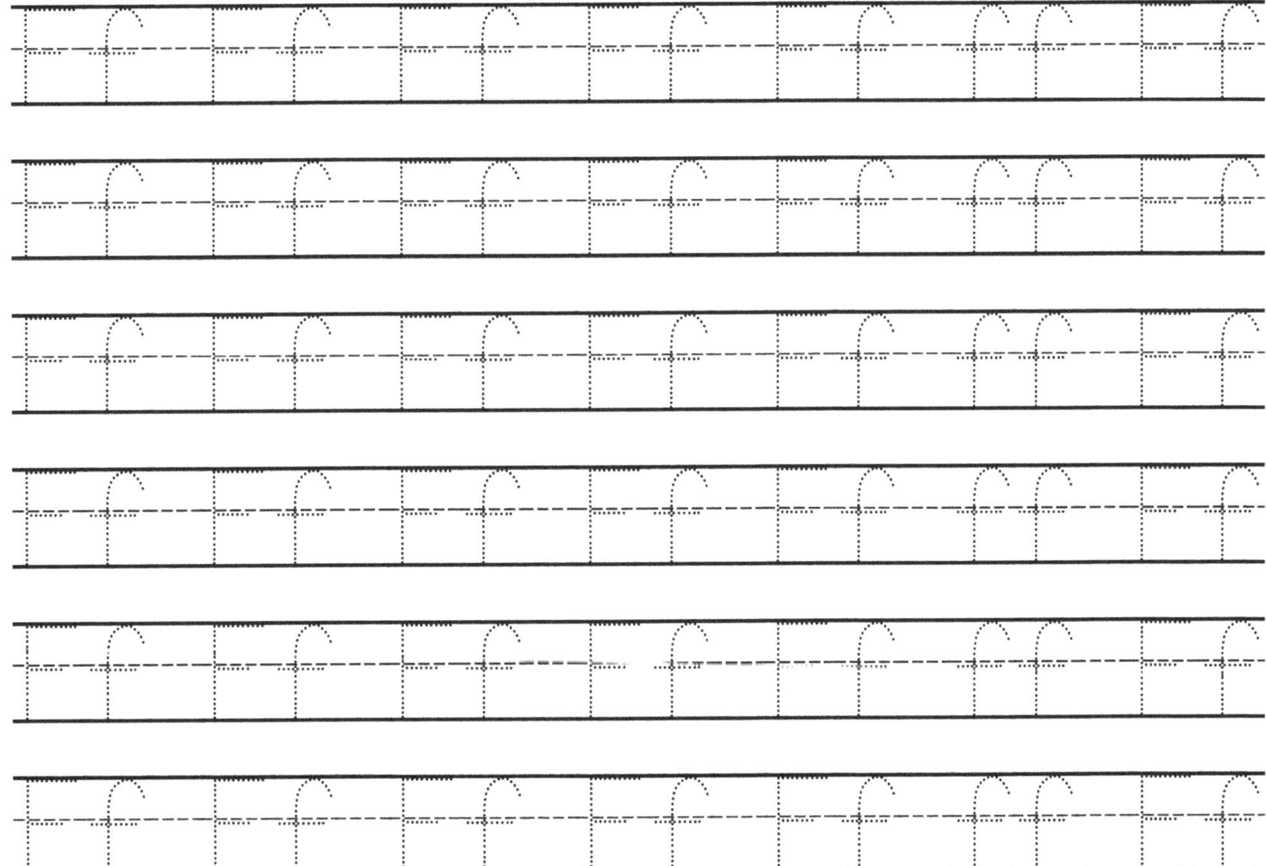

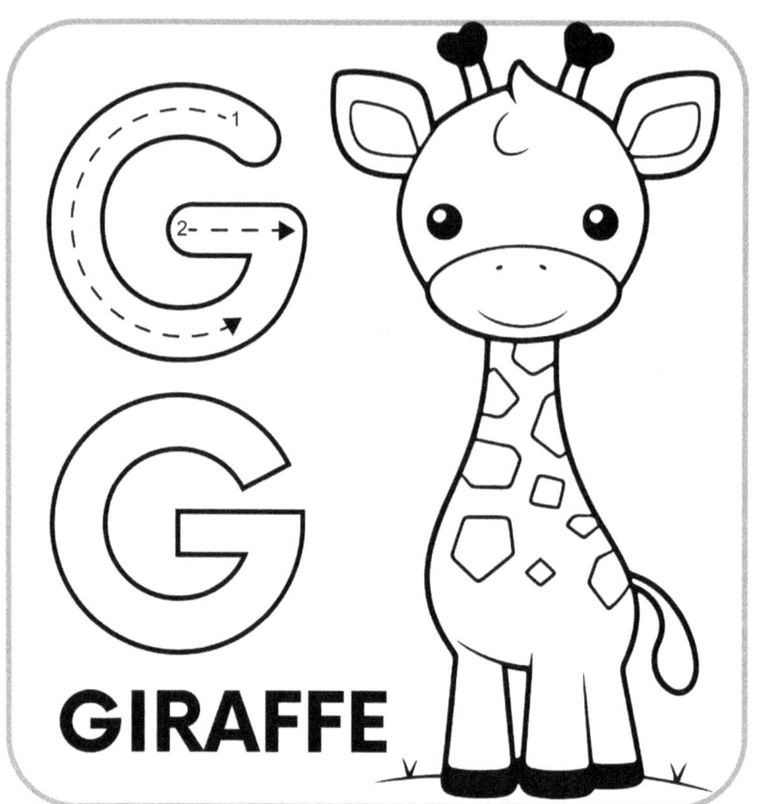

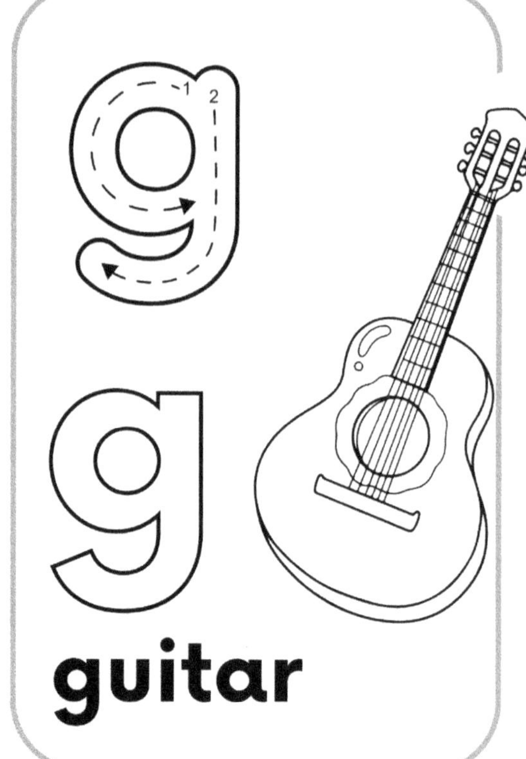

G

G

GIRAFFE

g

g

guitar

Gg Gg Gg Gg Gg Gg Gg

Gg Gg Gg Gg Gg Gg Gg

Gg Gg Gg Gg Gg Gg Gg

Gg Gg Gg Gg Gg Gg Gg

Gg Gg Gg Gg Gg Gg Gg

Gg Gg Gg Gg Gg Gg Gg

H H

HORSE

h h

house

Hh Hh Hh Hh Hh Hh Hh

Hh Hh Hh Hh Hh Hh Hh

Hh Hh Hh Hh Hh Hh Hh

Hh Hh Hh Hh Hh Hh Hh

Hh Hh Hh Hh Hh Hh Hh

Hh Hh Hh Hh Hh Hh Hh

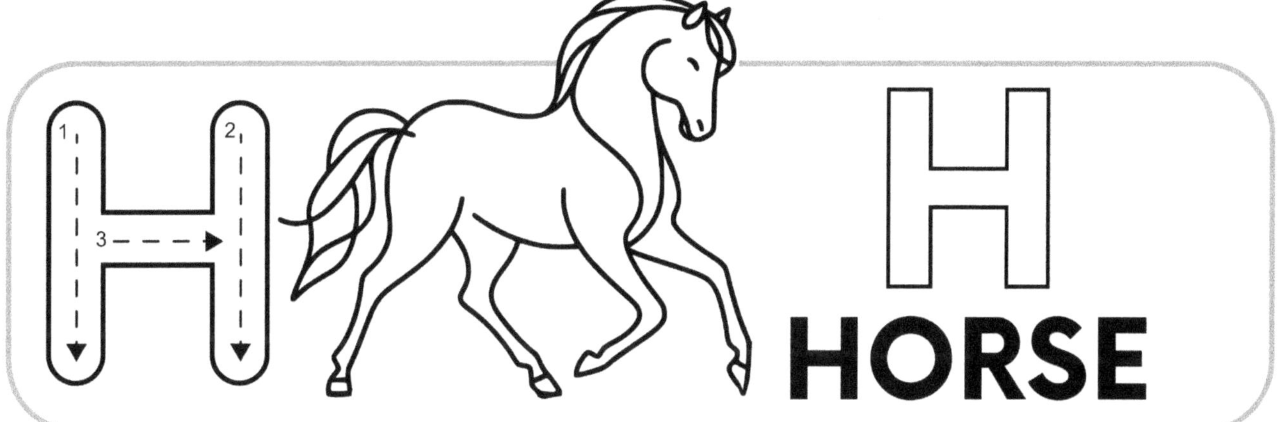

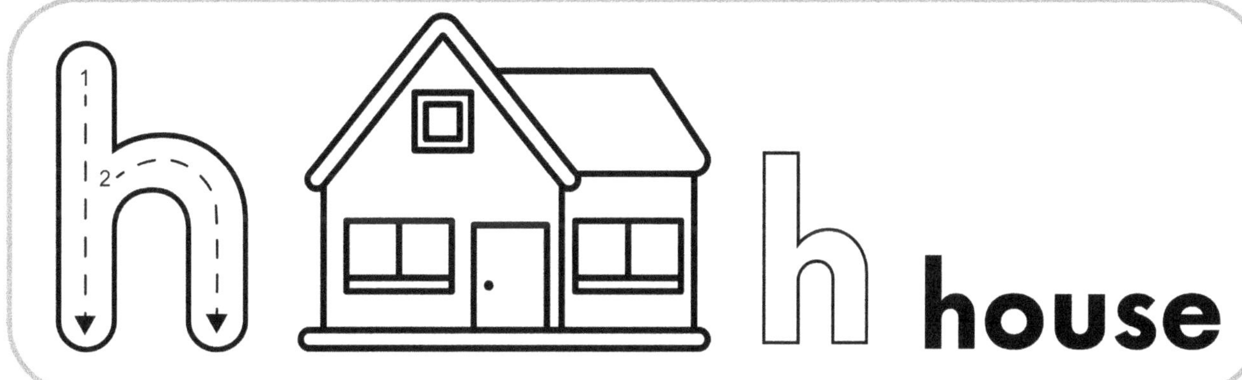

1
ICECREAM

2
1
insect

J
J
JEEP

j
j
jacket

K
1
2
3
K
KANGAROO
k
1
2
3
k
kite

L
LION
l
lemon

M
M
MONKEY
m
m
mango
Mm Mm Mm Mm Mm
Mm Mm Mm Mm Mm
Mm Mm Mm Mm Mm
Mm Mm Mm Mm Mm
Mm Mm Mm Mm Mm
Mm Mm Mm Mm Mm

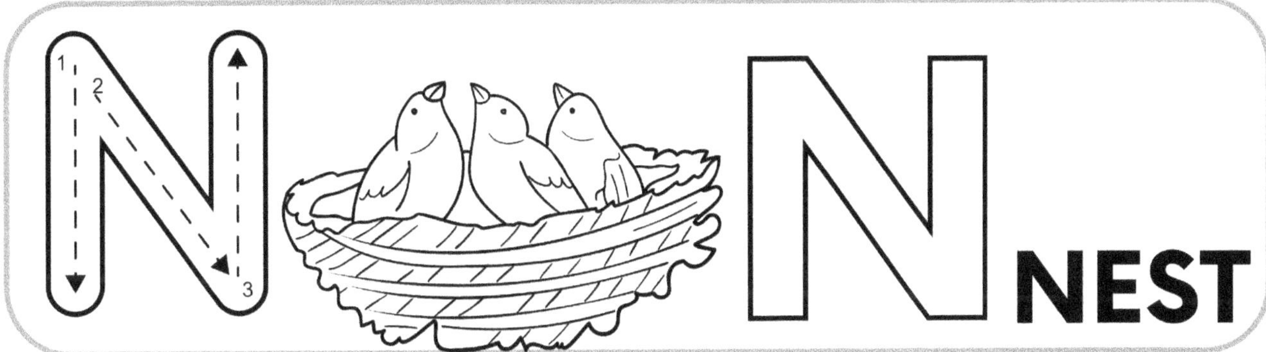

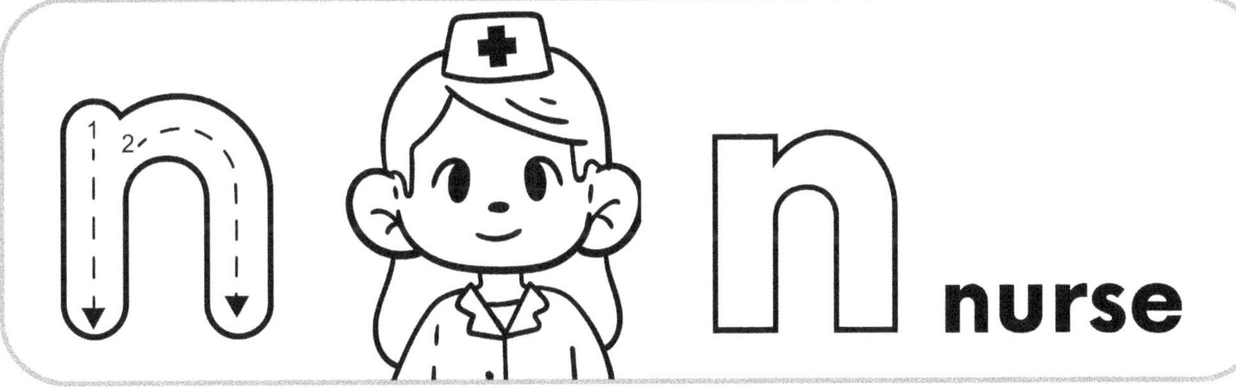

N N **NEST**

n n **nurse**

Nn Nn Nn Nn Nn Nn

Nn Nn Nn Nn Nn Nn

Nn Nn Nn Nn Nn Nn

Nn Nn Nn Nn Nn Nn

Nn Nn Nn Nn Nn Nn

Nn Nn Nn Nn Nn Nn

ostrich

P P **PARROT**

p p **pineapple**

Pp Pp Pp Pp Pp Pp

Pp Pp Pp Pp Pp Pp

Pp Pp Pp Pp Pp Pp

Pp Pp Pp Pp Pp Pp

Pp Pp Pp Pp Pp Pp

Pp Pp Pp Pp Pp Pp

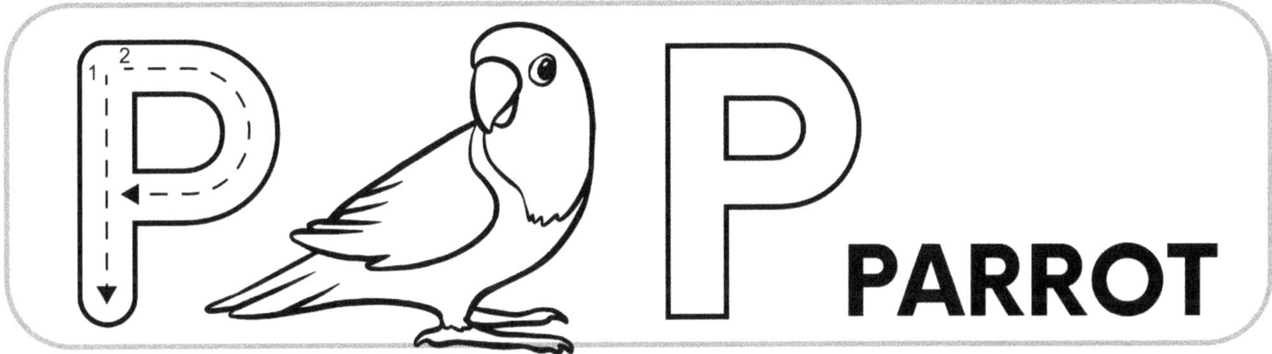

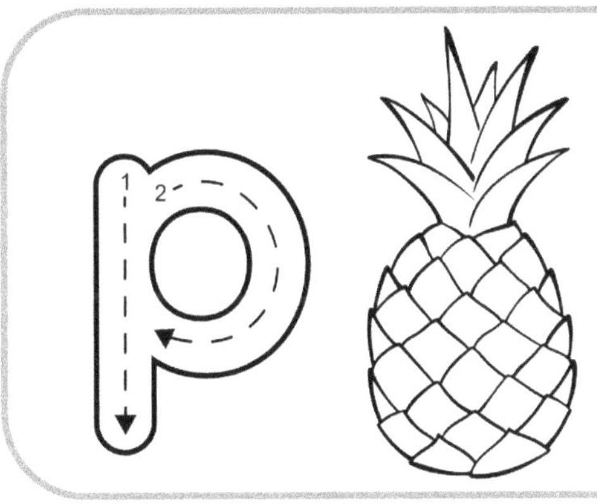

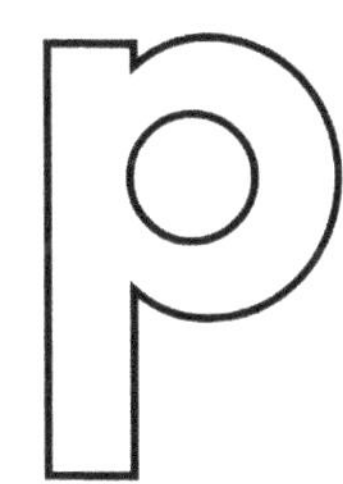

Q
QUEEN
q
quail

Rr Rr Rr Rr Rr Rr

Rr Rr Rr Rr Rr Rr

Rr Rr Rr Rr Rr Rr

Rr Rr Rr Rr Rr Rr

Rr Rr Rr Rr Rr Rr

Rr Rr Rr Rr Rr Rr

s

sunflower

S s S s S s S s S s S s

S s S s S s S s S s S s

S s S s S s S s S s S s

S s S s S s S s S s S s

S s S s S s S s S s S s

S s S s S s S s S s S s

2
1
T
TIGER

1
2
t
turtle

U

U

UMBRELLA

U

u

unicorn

1
2
V
VAN

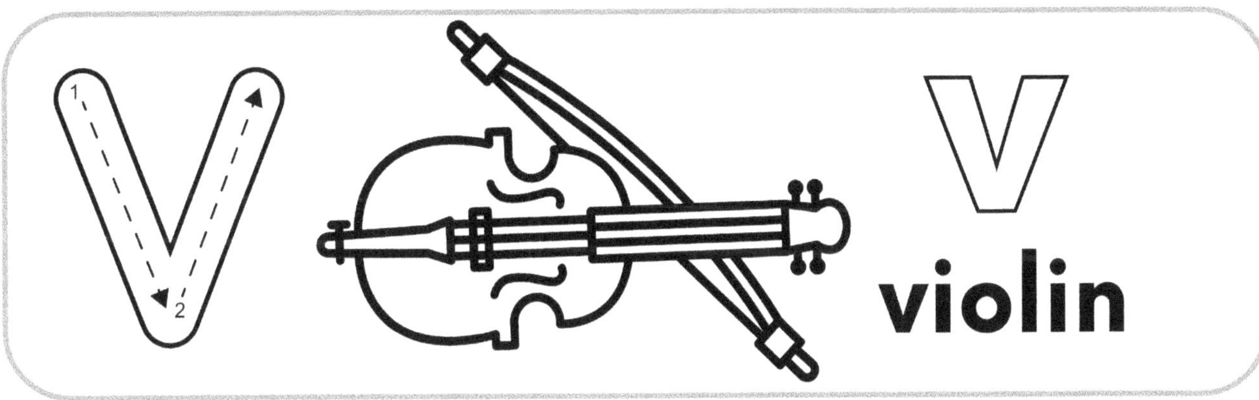

1
2
v
violin

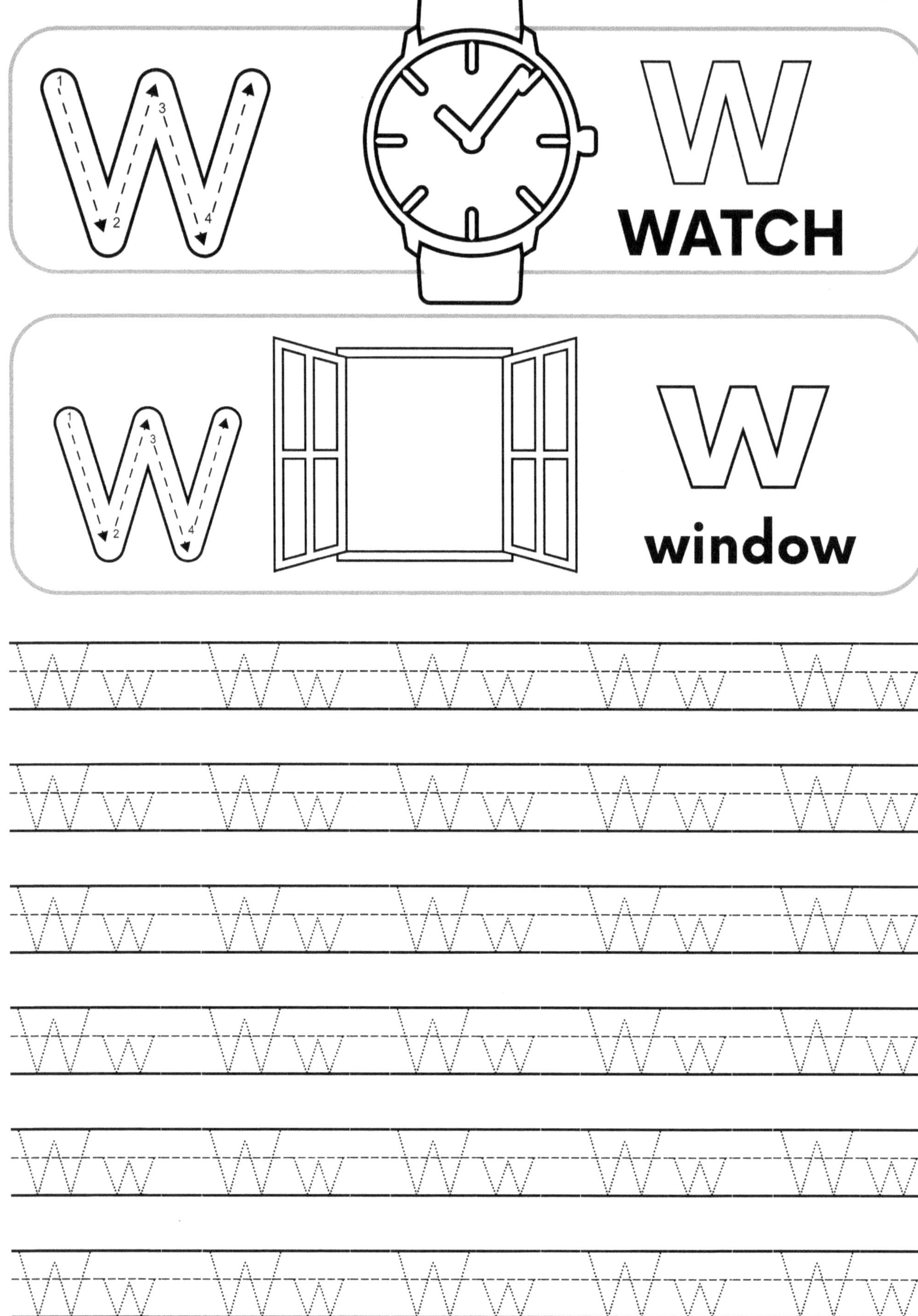
W
WATCH
w
window

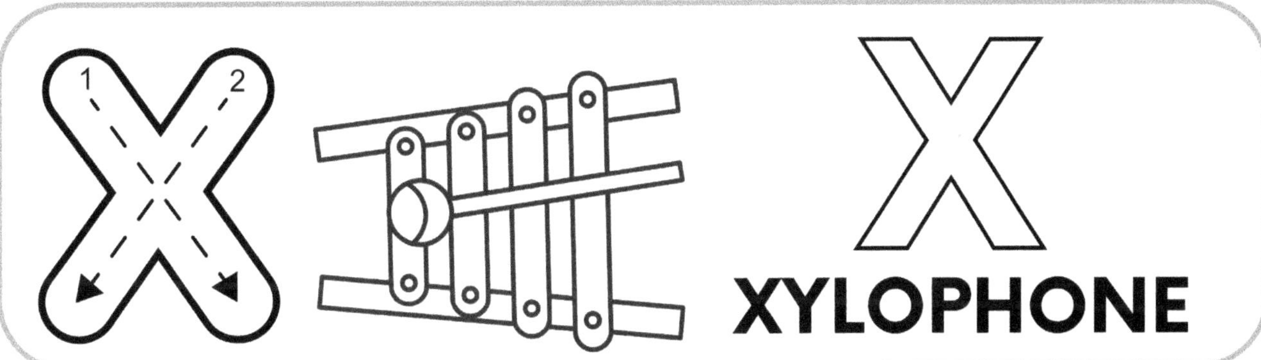
1
2
X
XYLOPHONE

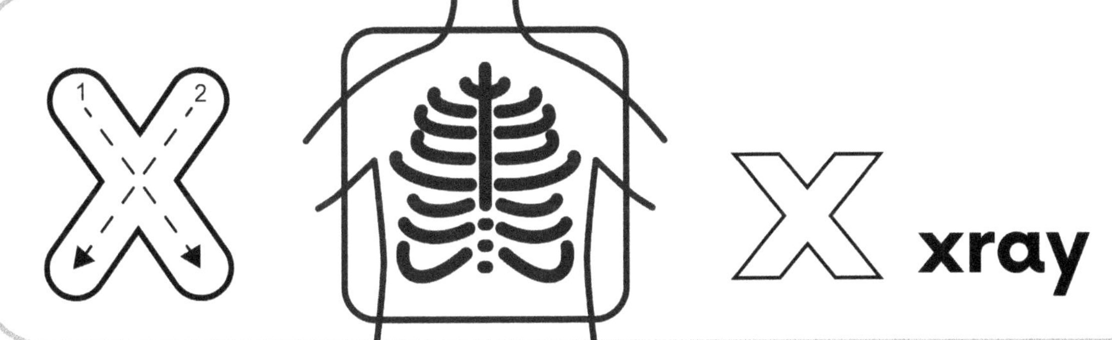
1
2
x
xray

Y
Y
YAK
y
y
yatch

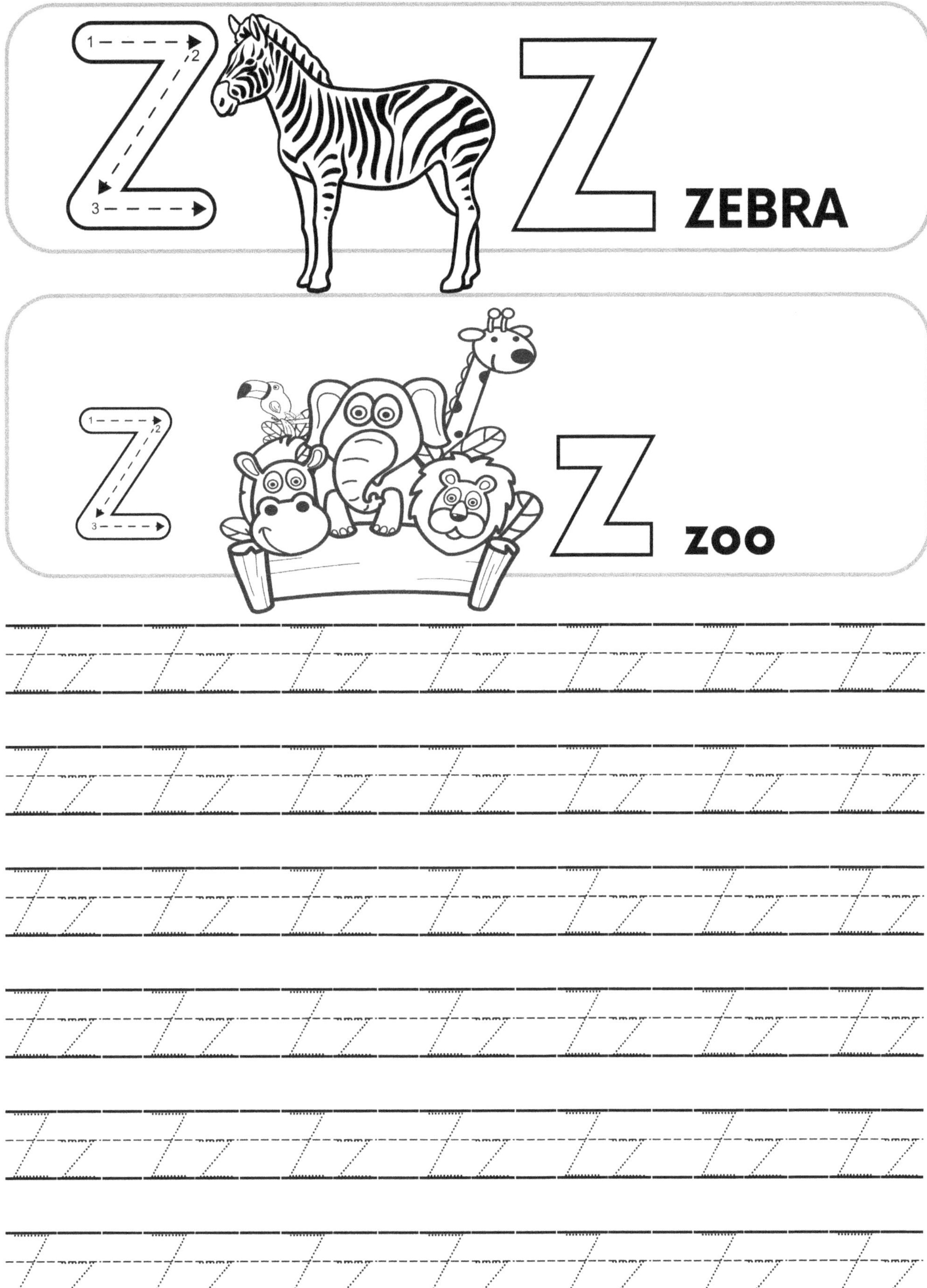

1
2
3
Z
ZEBRA
1
2
3
z
ZOO

Aa Bb Cc Dd
Ee Ff Gg Hh
Ii Jj Kk Ll
Mm Nn Oo Pp
Qq Rr Ss Tt
Uu Vv Ww Xx
Yy Zz

www.ingramcontent.com/pod-product-compliance
Lightning Source LLC
Chambersburg PA
CBHW040200110726
48005CB00018B/2832
* 9 7 9 8 8 9 5 1 9 0 4 8 7 *